My Bo...

by Anne Giulieri

Look at me.

This is my body.

3

This is my skin.
My skin is on the outside
of my body.

skin

I have bones.

My bones are on the inside of my body.

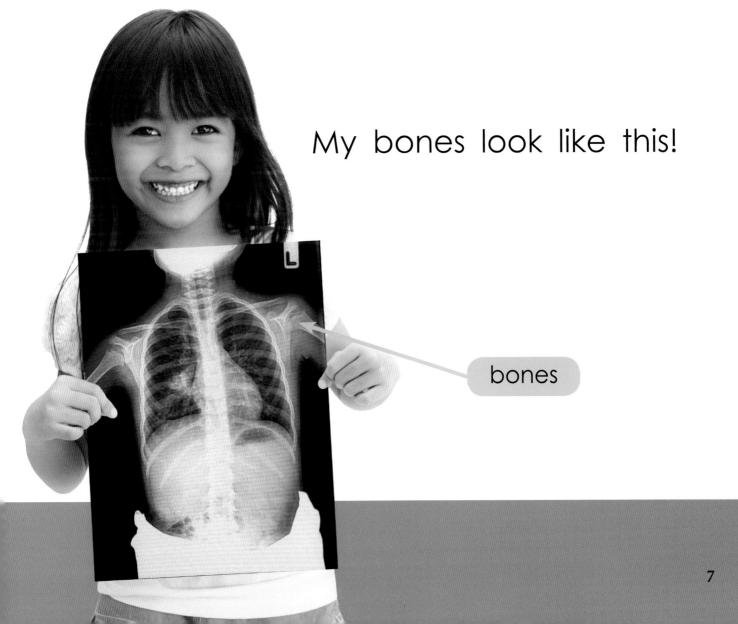

My bones look like this!

bones

I have 2 hands.
They help me to play
with my yellow ball.

Can you see my fingers?
I have 10 fingers.

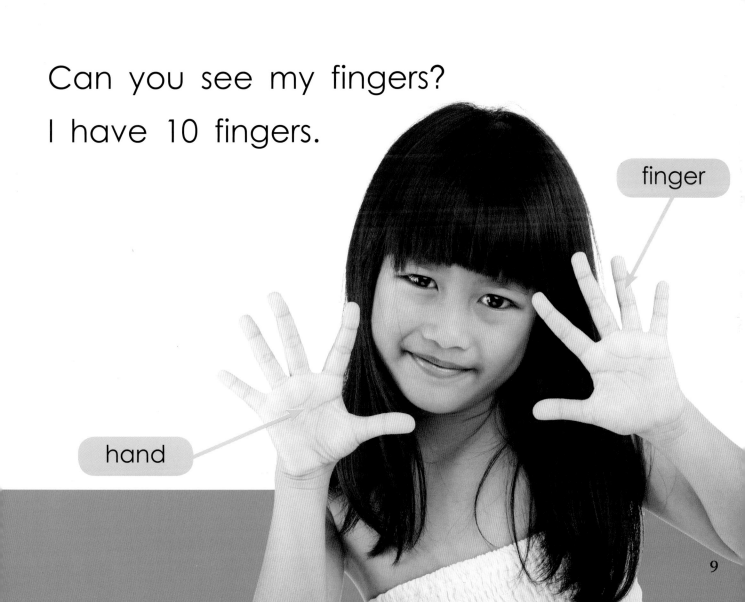

finger

hand

I have 2 legs and 2 feet.

They help me to run and play.

leg

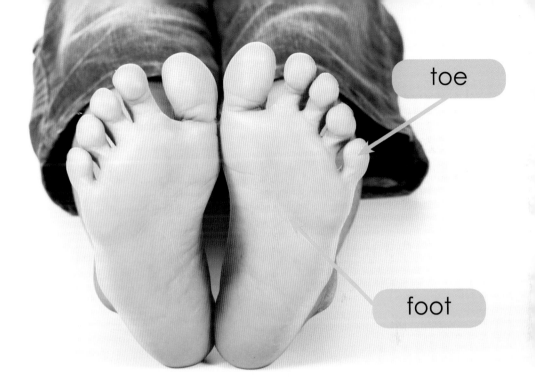

toe

foot

Can you see my toes?

I have 10 toes.

This is my face.

I have 2 brown eyes.
They help me to see.

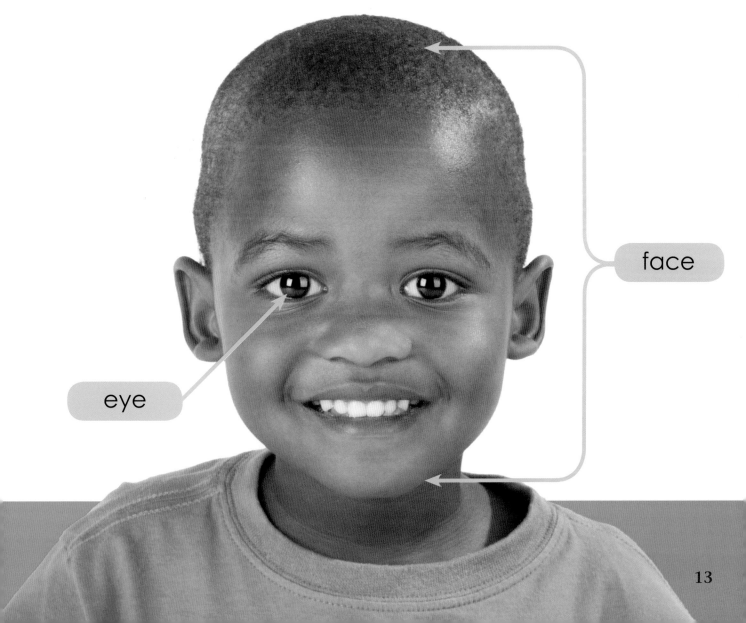

face

eye

13

Can you see my ears?

I have 2 ears.

They help me to hear.

ear

nose

I have a nose.

It helps me to smell.

I have a mouth too!
It helps me to eat.
Yum!

mouth